DR!VEN TO
SUCCEED

ARTISTS & ENTERTAINERS
WHO NEVER GAVE UP

BY
CHRIS SCHWAB

ILLUSTRATED BY
JOSHUA JANES

Rourke.

T0011695

1

Before Reading: *Building Background Knowledge and Vocabulary*

Building background knowledge can help children process new information and build upon what they already know. Before reading a book, it is important to tap into what children already know about the topic. This will help them develop their vocabulary and increase their reading comprehension.

Questions and Activities to Build Background Knowledge:

1. Look at the front cover of the book and read the title. What do you think this book will be about?
2. What do you already know about this topic?
3. Take a book walk and skim the pages. Look at the table of contents, photographs, captions, and bold words. Did these text features give you any information or predictions about what you will read in this book?

Vocabulary: *Vocabulary Is Key to Reading Comprehension*

Use the following directions to prompt a conversation about each word.

- Read the vocabulary words.
- What comes to mind when you see each word?
- What do you think each word means?

Vocabulary Words:
- committed
- cope
- dedicated
- determination
- obstacles
- option

During Reading: *Reading for Meaning and Understanding*

To achieve deep comprehension of a book, children are encouraged to use close reading strategies. During reading, it is important to have children stop and make connections. These connections result in deeper analysis and understanding of a book.

Close Reading a Text

During reading, have children stop and talk about the following:

- Any confusing parts
- Any unknown words
- Text to text, text to self, text to world connections
- The main idea in each chapter or heading

Encourage children to use context clues to determine the meaning of any unknown words. These strategies will help children learn to analyze the text more thoroughly as they read.

When you are finished reading this book, turn to the next-to-last page for **After-Reading Questions** and an **Activity**.

Table of Contents

The Art of Coping ↑

It's not easy to **cope** with challenges, but they teach us that we can learn new things and grow. Many artists and creators have responded courageously to challenges and painted a new world for themselves.

"Creativity takes courage."
Henri Matisse,
French visual artist

CHALLENGES AHEAD

Success did not come quickly or easily for SATOSHI TAJIRI, the Japanese video game designer who created Pokémon®. His unique game of collecting monsters encountered many challenges in the beginning.

POKÉMON

SATOSHI TAJIRI

PIKACHU

cope (kope): to deal with something effectively

5

In the beginning, Tajiri used his love of arcade games to create a magazine called *Game Freak*. But the more Tajiri wrote about video games, the more he wanted to make one. So he set out to design a video game loosely based on his childhood love of collecting bugs.

"When you're a kid and get your first bike, you want to go somewhere you've never been before."
**Satoshi Tajiri,
Japanese video game designer**

Over the next six years of trials and errors, Tajiri worked on perfecting his video game. He spent so much money on it, his magazine company almost went bankrupt. Only one company said yes to his game of collecting monsters—Nintendo®. Today, more than 1,000 creatures inhabit Pokémon World!

Cartoonist CHARLES SCHULZ gave us Charlie Brown, Snoopy, and the rest of the Peanuts gang. But early on, his drawings weren't popular. Every cartoon he drew for his high school yearbook was rejected. Good grief!

CHARLES SCHULZ

WHAT ARE YOU DOING HERE IN THE DOCTOR'S OFFICE, CHARLES?

I'M JUST HERE FOR A CHECKUP

NO! NEVER! NOT

HERE, YOU'RE SUPPOSED TO JUST SIT AND WORRY...

12-15

"To live is to dance, to dance is to live."
**Charles Schulz,
American cartoonist**

SNOOPY

All Schulz ever wanted to do was draw, so he stuck with it. As an adult, he took art classes and worked hard at becoming a better artist. Then, his cartoons started selling to magazines and newspapers. In 1950, the first *Peanuts* cartoon ran in seven newspapers across the country. His **determination** paid off!

A DISNEY LEGEND

Artist Retta Scott joined Disney Studios when women were only allowed to paint backgrounds. But Walt Disney saw her drawings and was impressed! He promoted her to drawing dogs for *Bambi*, and she made animation history by becoming the first woman to draw characters for a Disney movie.

determination (di-tur-muh-NAY-shuhn): a strong will to do something

Mexican artist FRIDA KAHLO spent a lot of time in a body cast after being injured in a bus accident when she was a teenager, but she did not take this setback lying down. Instead, she taught herself to paint in bed on an easel that fit over her lap.

FRIDA KAHLO

"Feet, what do I need you for when I have wings to fly?"
Frida Kahlo, Mexican artist

Kahlo turned her pain into art. Since she was often alone, she created a lot of self-portraits. Her love of Mexico inspired her to paint its culture too. Kahlo's fame grew slowly. She was well into her 40s when she had her first, and only, solo art exhibit one year before she died. Today, her paintings sell for millions of dollars. Kahlo is remembered for her bold colors, passionate portraits—and resilience.

WOMAN WITH A PARASOL

IMPRESSIONS OF AN ARTIST

Painter Claude Monet's art was mocked and rejected by art galleries during his early career. His paintings didn't sell, and sometimes he didn't have enough money for painting supplies. But he was courageous and driven enough to keep painting. Today, Monet's paintings are some of the most famous in the world.

The Comeback Awards ↑

Everyone encounters setbacks, but people with determination turn them into comebacks. These actors turned hard knocks into opportunities for success by reaching for the stars. Their stars led them to Hollywood and YouTube fame. Your stars can lead you … anywhere!

STEVEN HE

Meet STEVEN HE, social media star. At age 11, he dreamed of becoming a child actor. But when he auditioned for TV shows, He rarely got hired. So he took acting lessons.

Years filled with rejection passed, but He was **committed**. He applied for 20 acting roles every morning. After being turned down 3,000 times by age 25, He took matters into his own hands. He created a role for himself in his very own show—on his cell phone!

"After studying hundreds of videos and collecting hundreds of channels worth of data, I figured out a few things. But it still took me 220 videos before I got significant views."
Steven He, Chinese-born Irish actor, comedian, social media personality

He's genius idea was to make videos on TikTok that mirrored his own Asian-American family life. Viewers loved it! He soon had so many followers he switched to the more popular YouTube. Thirteen million followers later, He has achieved his dream of starring in movies and TV shows.

committed (kuh-MIT-ted): made a promise to

Award-winning actress HALLE BERRY's life has not always been glamorous. Before achieving fame and stardom, she first had to overcome years of sickness, abuse, abandonment, homelessness, and racism. None of these **obstacles** stopped her.

obstacles (AHB-stuh-kuhlz): things that make it difficult to do or achieve something

"Don't take yourself too seriously."
Halle Berry,
American actress

HALLE
BERRY

As a young adult, Berry worked hard to get acting experience. At one point, she was broke and living in a homeless shelter while auditioning for acting roles. Her first major TV role was cancelled. As she got more TV and movie roles, her reputation as a talented actor grew. In 2002, she was the first African American woman to win an Academy Award for Best Actress in a movie. Berry says giving up was never an **option**.

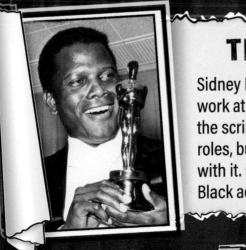

SIDNEY POITIER

TRULY A COMEBACK KID

Sidney Poitier grew up poor and had to leave school to work at age 12. He wanted to act but could barely read the scripts. He was constantly passed over for acting roles, but Poitier took rejection as a challenge and stuck with it. In 1964, at the age of 37, he became the first Black actor to win an Academy Award for Best Actor.

option (AHP-shuhn): a choice

Winning Stories ↑

Hard work is the first ingredient in the recipe for success. It builds character and self-esteem but also prepares people for the race ahead. Ask these writers, who faced rejection and frustration, but crossed the finish line with flying colors.

"What separates the talented individual from the successful one is a lot of hard work."
Stephen King,
American author

Author STEPHEN KING spent most of first grade at home sick with measles, strep throat, and ear infections. He read lots of comic books to pass the time. Eventually he would start writing his own books.

STEPHEN KING

Once King started writing, he didn't stop. He was **dedicated**. In college, he sold his first story for $35.

A few years later, while working two jobs, he began writing his first novel. One late night, while struggling with it, he angrily crumpled it up and threw it in the trash.

iT

"Hope is the thing with feathers – That perches in the soul – And sings the tune without the words – And never stops – at all"
Emily Dickinson, American poet

King's wife retrieved the pages and encouraged him to keep writing. She knew he had a good story to tell.

He went back to work on his novel titled *Carrie*. Although rejected by 30 publishers when finished, *Carrie* became one of his most famous and best-selling books and movies. King's dedication has helped him write more than 60 worldwide best-selling novels.

HOPE IS THE THING

Beloved poet Emily Dickinson lived with sadness, loss—but also hope. She was often ill, suffered from epilepsy, and missed a lot of school. So, she wrote poems. Even though only 10 of her 1,800 poems were published in her lifetime, she is known as one of the greatest poets of all time.

Emily Dickinson
U.S. 8c
American Poet

dedicated (DED-i-kate-ed): to give a lot of time and energy to something

After suffering terrible abuse as a young girl, MAYA ANGELOU stopped talking for five years. Her grandmother brought her books of poems, and Angelou memorized poem after poem. It was hard work finding her words, but the words of others gave her a voice again. A poet was born.

1993 PRESIDENTIAL INAUGURATION

"Nothing will work unless you do."
Dr. Maya Angelou, American poet

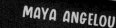
MAYA ANGELOU

Angelou had a lot to say throughout her lifetime, despite the continuing abuse and racism. She wrote seven autobiographies, three books of essays, and several books of poetry. In 1993, she read one of her most famous poems at President Clinton's inauguration. Angelou not only found her words—she shared them for the world to enjoy.

CHECK THE CLOSET!

C.S. Lewis, the British author of *The Chronicles of Narnia*, faced 800 rejections before his first book was published. He wrote 40 more books and is one of the most influential writers of the 20th century.

People often say, "Never give up!" This is easier said than done. To persevere, it helps to focus on a goal, like these famous musicians did who faced failure again and again. Making music can be hard work.

NEVER GIVE UP

Singer-songwriter BEYONCÉ KNOWLES entered dance and singing competitions at age seven. She was often the only Black girl, and she felt she had to work twice as hard to get noticed. When her Girl's Tyme band competed on a TV talent show in 1992, they lost. They were later dropped from a recording contract before their album was ever released. But they didn't give up.

DESTINY'S CHILD

Girl's Tyme, which became Destiny's Child, persisted for nearly eight years. But Beyoncé's musical career was unsteady. She struggled with severe vocal injury and depression. Despite her setbacks, Beyoncé launched her first solo album in 2003. Destiny's Child broke up a few years later.

"If everything was perfect, you would never learn, and you would never grow."
Beyoncé Knowles, American singer, songwriter

BEYONCÉ

Beyoncé kept her eye on the prize—and won a lot of them! She became the first Black and youngest woman to win the Songwriter of the Year award. Her first solo album won five Grammy Awards. "Queen Bey" became the queen of Grammys in 2023, with a record 32 wins.

COME TOGETHER

The Beatles were a British rock band that never quit despite countless rejections. One recording studio said guitar groups were out-of-date. Record labels turned them down. So they brought their music to America, and crowds went wild. The Beatles sold several hundred million records worldwide.

Singer and actor ELVIS PRESLEY got his first guitar for his 11th birthday in 1946. As a shy child who was often bullied by classmates, Presley loved playing his guitar and singing. His eighth-grade music teacher, however, said he had no talent.

"When I was a child, ladies and gentlemen, I was a dreamer."
**Elvis Presley,
American singer,
songwriter, actor**

ELVIS
PRESLEY

With the courage to compete in his high school's talent show, Presley shocked everyone with his voice. A star was born!

Just a few years later, Presley's popularity exploded with his first hit single, "Heartbreak Hotel." The hip-swinging "King of Rock and Roll" went on to sell more than a billion records worldwide and starred in 33 movies—all because of his "burning love" for music.

I WISH

Stevie Wonder lost his sight at just six weeks old. Amazingly, he learned to play the harmonica, drums, and piano by age 10. During his legendary career, he won 25 Grammy Awards and a spot in the Rock & Roll Hall of Fame.

STEVIE WONDER

Memory Game

Look at the pictures. Can you retell their stories?

Index

After-Reading Questions

1. What did these creative people have in common?

2. Which creative person do you admire most? Give two reasons why.

3. What is the difference between people who quit and people who keep going?

4. Why do you think Halle Berry felt that giving up was not an option?

5. Tell a friend about a time you were able to keep your eye on the prize, as Beyoncé did.

Activity

Write a letter to your future self to open in one month, one year, or longer. Tell yourself about a goal you want to reach. List the steps you think are needed to achieve that goal. List obstacles you expect to encounter along the way. Suggest strategies to overcome them. Keep the letter in a safe place and open it when the time comes. Did you achieve your goal?

About the Author

Chris Schwab is a former teacher and writer currently living in Greensboro, North Carolina. Her life's dream since a child was to become an author. She read books, wrote lots of stories, and took writing classes. She persevered and now has the pleasure of creating books for a living.

About the Illustrator

Joshua Janes' love of drawing and his family's support lent him the resilience, tenacity, and perseverance needed to obtain a career as an illustrator from his studio in Ohio.

www.rourkebooks.com

PHOTO CREDITS ©: cover: Graham Whitby/Allstar/Sportsphoto Ltd./Allstar/Newscom; cover: Valerie Loiseleux/GettyImages; cover: FOTOKITA/GettyImages; cover: merovingian/GettyImages; cover: AlexRoz/Shutterstock; cover: He2/GettyImages; cover: Splash News/Newscom; cover: Jeff Whyte/Shutterstock; cover: Ned Snowman/Shutterstock; pg all: serts/GettyImages; pg all: mouu007/GettyImages; pg all: Paladin12/Shutterstock; pg all: robbin lee/Shutterstock; pg all: grafius/Shutterstock; pg 1: merovingian/GettyImages; pg 1: AlexRoz/Shutterstock; pg 3: ESB Professional/Shutterstock; pg 3: Carlos E. Santa Maria/Shutterstock; pg 4: Carlos E. Santa Maria/Shutterstock; pg 4: amanalang/GettyImages; pg 4: fotodelux/GettyImages; pg 5: hakanyalicn/Shutterstock; pg 5: Kyodo News/Newscom; pg 5: DPST/Newscom; pg 5: enjoynz/GettyImages; pg5: Kyodo News/Newscom; pg 5: Flas100/Shutterstock; pg 5: Flas100/Shutterstock; pg 6: Hakase_/GettyImages; pg 6: Maridav/Shutterstock; pg 7: KeongDaGreat/Shutterstock; pg 7: Hethers/Shutterstock; pg 7: J.Papagoda Photo/Shutterstock; pg 8: Everett Collection/Newscom; pg 8: Dave Kennedy / iPhoto Inc./Newscom; pg 8: Claire Doherty/Sipa USA/Newscom; pg 9: Macrobyte/Shutterstock; pg 10: Salvatore Esposito/Pacific Press/Newscom; pg 10: Salvatore Esposito/ZUMAPRESS/Newscom; pg 11: Album/Newscom; pg 11: ZaharovEvgeniy/GettyImages; pg 12: Sataporn Sakda/Shutterstock; pg 13: jgroup/GettyImages; pg 13: Kirk Wester/GettyImages; pg 13: SYSPEO/SIPA/Newscom; pg 14: lchumpitaz; pg 14: iamnoonmai/GettyImages; pg 14: fotostorm/GettyImages; pg 15: Flas100/Shutterstock; pg 15: Nuad Contributor/Shutterstock; pg 15: Issarawat Tattong/Shutterstock; pg 16: Andrew Hobbs/GettyImages; pg 16: Author WENN / WENN English Top Features/Newscom; pg 17: Carlos E. Santa Maria/Shutterstock; pg 17: Austral Press Agency/ZUMAPRESS/Newscom; pg 18: sirtravelalot/Shutterstock; pg 19: Flas100/Shutterstock; pg 19: VARLEY/SIPA/Newscom; pg 19: hamdi bendali/Shutterstock; pg 19: hamdi bendali/Shutterstock; pg 20: Richard B. Levine/Newscom; pg 20: Luke W Bryant/Shutterstock; pg 20: 1000WordsPhotos/Shutterstock; pg 20: Eyesonmilan/Shutterstock; pg 21: catwalker/Shutterstock; pg 21: Carlos E. Santa Maria/Shutterstock; pg 22: Arnie Sachs - CNP/picture alliance/Consolidated News Photos/Newscom; pg 22: Everett Collection/Newscom; pg 23: WALT DISNEY PICTURES/Album/Newscom; pg 24: Khosro/Shutterstock; pg 24: Gustavo Frazao/Shutterstock; pg 25: Russell Einhorn/Splash News/Newscom; pg 26: PacificCoastNews/Newscom; pg 26: RHA/ZOB/WENN/Newscom; pg 27: RichartPhotos/Shutterstock; pg 27: Carlos E. Santa Maria/Shutterstock; pg 28: MIRISCH/UNITED ARTISTS / Album/Newscom; pg 28: billyhoiler/GettyImages; pg 28: LPETTET/GettyImages; pg 28: insjoy/Gettyimages; pg 28: christopher krohn/Shutterstock; pg 29: Carlos E. Santa Maria/Shutterstock; pg 29: A.PAES/Shutterstock

QUOTE SOURCES: pg 4: brainyquote.com; pg 6: azquotes.com; pg 8: allgreatquotes.com; pg 10: oprahdaily.com; pg 14: forbes.com; pg 16: brainyquote.com; pg 18: medium.com; pg 20: goodreads.com; pg 22: brainyquote.com; pg 24: graceland.com

Edited by: Catherine Malaski   Cover & interior design/illustration by: Joshua Janes

Library of Congress PCN Data

Artists & Entertainers Who Never Gave Up / Chris Schwab
(Driven to Succeed)
ISBN 978-1-73165-771-8 (hard cover) (alk. paper)
ISBN 978-1-73165-782-4 (e-book)
Library of Congress Control Number: 2023942368

ISBN 978-1-73165-780-0 (soft cover)
ISBN 978-1-73165-784-8 (e-pub)

Rourke Educational Media
Printed in the United States of America
01-0152411937